W9-ABC-517

CONTENTS

Christmas

Thanksgiving

Standard

Christmas

Program

Book

Number 47

compiled by

Laurie Hoard

cover photo by

Bob Taylor

STANDARD PUBLISHING
Cincinnati, Ohio   8647

Unless otherwise noted, all Scripture quotations in this publication are from the Holy Bible, *New International Version.* Copyright 1973, 1978, 1984 International Bible Society. Used by permission of Zondervan Bible Publishers.

ISBN O-87239-935-4

Copyright 1986 The STANDARD PUBLISHING Company,
Cincinnati, Ohio.
A division of STANDEX INTERNATIONAL Corporation.
Printed in U.S.A.

OLD BUT TRUE

Phyllis Michael

I have a little wish that's
As old as old can be;
But then I truly mean it
I'm sure you all can see.*

*(Holds up an aged card, perhaps
torn at edges, reading "MERRY
CHRISTMAS.")

WHY WE HAVE CHRISTMAS

Lois Sink

In a lowly stable
Filled with sweet and fragrant hay,
God's holy Son, the child divine,
Was born on Christmas Day.

DOUBLE WISHES

Helen Evans

My teacher asked me to say,
"Have a happy Christmas Day!"
That's for her—this one's from me,
(pauses)
Have a new year filled with glee!

OPEN EVERY HEART

Robert Colbert

Open, open, every heart,
Welcome, welcome, little Lord;
God sends down from Heaven
above
Christ His Son, His gift of love.

THE CHRISTMAS STORY

Lois Sink

'Tis the old, old story of Christmas,
Old, yet ever new,
That fills our souls with gladness
Our faith and hope renew.

MY SHARE

Phyllis Michael

I wish that I could play a song
Or sing like some folks do;
But I'm too little, so you see
This card is meant for you.

(Holds up card reading "Merry Christmas.")

CHRIST IS BORN

Robert Colbert

Christ is born!
Christ is born!
Sons of men and angels say,
"Welcome, welcome
Christmas Day!"

WHY JESUS CAME

Lois Sink

Life holds no sweeter joy than this,
To tell of Jesus' birth,
And how He came from Heaven
above
To save all men on earth.

HE LIVES

Donna Maness

I did not hear the angels
Sing or play upon their harps;
But I know Jesus lives because
He lives in my heart.

MY GIFT TO HIM

Phyllis Michael

My heart is so very small
But take it, Jesus, take it all;
And may it make Your Christmas
  bright,
That's all I ask this Christmas night.

THE STAR

Lois Sink

The star that led the Wise-men
  To where the Christ child lay,
Will lead us onward, upward
  To Heaven some glad day.

A LITTLE BOY

Donna Maness

Jesus was a little boy
Like me, I guess,
He came to bring people
Lots of happiness.

HAPPY NEW YEAR

Nona Duffy

Happy voices now are singing,
  And the New Year has begun;
Joyful bells are brightly ringing,
  Happy New Year, everyone!

PRACTICE MAKES PERFECT

Phyllis Michael

I've said my part
  Again and again;
"Peace on earth
  Good will to men."

WELCOME EVERYONE

Donna Maness

Welcome everyone, neighbors and
  Friends so kind and true;
We're here tonight to tell you
  That Jesus loves you, too!

A PRAYER OF PRAISE

Lois Sink

Dear Lord, accept the praise we bring
  With grateful hearts of love;
For giving us the best you had—
  Your Son, sent from above.

THE BEST DATE

Helen Evans

Lots of months are pleasant
  But December 25's the best date
For that's the time of Jesus' birth
  And all Christians celebrate.

A PRAYER FOR CHRISTMAS

Lois Sink

We praise You and we worship You
  In prayer and song just now;
With grateful and loving hearts joyfully
  come,
  We before You humbly bow.

MEDIUM

IT'S CHRISTMAS DAY
Nona Duffy

All the world
  Is glad to say
That once again
  It's Christmas Day!

Years ago,
  One silent night,
A star shone down
  With splendid light!

And gentle Mary,
  Gracious lady,
Gave the world
  Her precious baby!

Joy is here
  On Christmas morn,
Because the infant
  Christ was born!

A NEW YEAR PRAYER
Helen Evans

We come to You for the days ahead,
  For strength of spirit and power,
For the ability to follow You
  Every single hour.

For strength of body and mind
  For we are very frail;
Hold each hand and lead us
  So that we shall not fail.

Bless our efforts with success,
  Sustain us with Your love;
Make us ever mindful, Lord,
  That all blessings come from above.

THAT'S WHY
Phyllis Michael

Yes, there really is a Savior,
  He's the light, the truth, the way;
Christ came down from Heaven to
  save us,
  That's why there's a Christmas Day.

CHRISTMAS TREE
Nona Duffy

We have a tree
  With branches green,
And bright blue lights
  Looped in between.

We've hung some tinsel
  From each bough;
It's red and green
  And silver now!

CHRISTMAS
Edith Hafley

Christmas means lots of
  things to people everywhere:
Some think of only presents
  and gifts that they may share.
But when I think of Christmas,
  I think of God above,
And how He sent us Jesus and
  His everlasting love.

A MESSAGE OF LOVE
Donna Maness

I didn't bring a present
  Or a gift of any kind,
But I bring a message
  For all mankind.
The message is simple and true,
God loves me and you.

ISN'T IT NICE?

Helen Evans

Isn't it nice to have a church
  Where we can gather and see
All our friends and loved ones
  In our community?

Isn't it nice at Christmas
  To hear the Christmas story
Of Jesus and His birth
  And of God's great glory?

Isn't it nice at Christmas
  To know a baby's birth
Brought love for all mankind
  To share throughout the earth?

CHRISTMAS BELLS

Nona Duffy

I love the bells
  That ring or chime
And stir my heart
  At Christmastime!

What joy to me
  The carols bring,
When carolers
  Begin to sing.

But best of all
  I like the cheer
Of Christmas bells
  When they ring clear!

And when I hear
  The chiming start
They make sweet music
  In my heart!

A HAPPY TIME

Helen Evans

Christmastime is a happy time,
  We're happy as can be;
It seems our family's closer
  As we gather 'round the tree.

We sing the Christmas carols
  And read the Bible story;
We renew once again
  The feeling of His glory.

Christmas is a happy time
  For all upon the earth
Because it is the time
  To celebrate Christ's birth.

MY THANKS FOR CHRISTMAS

Phyllis Michael

Once long ago on Christmas night
A wondrous star shone clear and brig
Away above a lonely stall
To bring a message to us all.
It told the world a blessed king
Had come at last, His peace to bring.
Wise-men came with gifts so rare
And knelt before the Christ child ther
Oh, thank You, God, for Christmas Da
And all it means in every way!
You sent Your Son from Heaven above
Oh, thank You, God, for all Your love.

CHRISTMASTIME!

Phyllis Michael

Christmastime! Christmastime!
  Every church bell rings;
Christmastime! Christmastime!
  And here's the word each brings:
"Christ was born on Christmas Day
  Very long ago;
He came to save us from our sins
  Because He loves us so."

IT'S CATCHING

Helen Evans

Smile at all you see,
It's catching as can be;
Be kind to others every day
It's catching when you live this way.

At this season of the year
Give happiness to those you're near;
Smile a lot and you will see
That Christmas is catching as can
  be!

GLAD TIDINGS

Eldreth Russell

Gladsome tidings angels brought
  When Jesus Christ was born;
And joyous messages we sing
  On every Christmas morn.

This joyous news we share today
  About the Savior's birth;
For God was spreading happiness
  When Jesus came to earth.

WELCOME THE NEW YEAR!

Nona Duffy

Welcome the new year!
  Let the bells ring;
Lift up your voices,
  Everyone sing!

The new year is here,
  Start it off right;
Bid it good fortune
  And welcome tonight!

The old year is passing,
  There's no one to mourn!
We are rejoicing
  For the new year is born!

I'M IMPORTANT

Helen Evans

Why is it when something is
  important
  They always call my name?
Perhaps with all my speaking
  I'm winning lots of fame!
Well, anyway, I'm here again
  To say to each of you,
Merry, Merry Christmas
  And a Happy New Year, too!

(For a child who appears often on programs.)

BE NEAR

Phyllis Michael

"Dear Christ, be born again today
Within my heart," this prayer I pray.
"Oh, keep me pure and clean within
And free from every kind of sin.
Walk with me through the coming
   year;
Be always very, very near."

JESUS' BIRTH

Helen Evans

The shepherds were watching their
   sheep
   When they heard of Jesus' birth;
Jesus, our Savior, was born
   He had been sent to earth.

The shepherds heard the good news
   And they shouted for great joy!
Jesus had come to earth
   As a tiny baby boy.

ALL THINGS FOR GOOD

Phyllis Michael

I wonder why can't Christmas come
   When things are warm and nice?
My nose is cold and I'm sure my feet
   Have turned to chunks of ice.

But I think it must be very plain
   To God, in fact I'm sure,
He does all things for our own good
   And the cold I'll just endure.

A GOOD CHRISTMAS

Helen Evans

Friends are the best part of Christmas,
   Friends with whom you share
The happiness togetherness brings,
   Friends who really care.

Christian friends who love Jesus,
   Who try each day to live right;
This is what makes a good Christmas,
   A day that is cheerful and bright.

DIFFICULT

ONE CANDLE

Helen Evans

One candle proclaims the light of the world!
  Let us light it with love and with care;
Let us light it for peace and for love,
  May it shine in the world every-where.

May the faith and the patience of Jesus
  Be our companions as well,
May the spirit of Christmas abide,
  May its message forever swell.

May we greet the tomorrows with singing
  When all hate in the world will be gone;
May that candle we light be burning
  Each day as we face a new dawn.

THE SEASONS

Katherine Peavy

Springtime's my favorite season,
  And here's the reason why;
The winter's gone, the hills are green
  And everywhere, flowers glorify.

But, maybe summertime's the best,
  And this is why, you see
There's swimming, hikes, and picnics, too,
  They're all such joy for me.

But in the autumn leaves are falling
  And it's apple-picking time;
Autumn's such a lovely season
  That I can't make up my mind!

But now that winter's come to stay
  It's the best time of the year;
With all the jolly holidays
  To share with families dear.

So, which season is my favorite?
  Why my favorite's every one!
For each one has its own delights
  And its special kind of fun.

THE LEGEND OF THE TREES

Katherine Peavy

Three trees grew on a hillside bare
Each with a vision of its future there.
Said the first, "I would be a bed
Where a tiny child might lay his head."
Said the second, "I a tall ship's mast would be
And sail the oceans forever free."
Said the third, "I am content to stand
Here on the hillside and grace the land."
The first tree became a cattle stall
And in it, a crib for a baby small.
The second tree felled by the woods-men, then
Became a boat for the fishers of men.
But the third tree that chose on the hill to abide
Became the cross where our Savior died.

11

IT'S UP TO US

Helen Evans

The joyful bells of Christmas
  Are still ringing in each ear;
But now I hear them saying
  "It's here! A brand new year!"

A brand new year for doing
  The things that may help bring
    peace;
The things that may cause wars
  We may help forever cease.

A brand new year of thinking
  Of others more each day;
A brand new year to set aside
  More time to worship and pray.

A brand new year is given us,
  How we use it we decide;
Let's walk in Christian ways
  Filled with true Christian pride.

A NEW YEAR

Helen Evans

May the new year find you
  Filled with love and cheer;
Surrounded by good friends
  And those you hold most dear.

May it give you renewed strength
  To face the days ahead;
May you have new inspiration
  For the tasks that you may dread.

May there be new avenues for
    service,
  New ways to show greater love;
May you have God's blessings
  Showered on you from above.

IN FAR OFF JUDEA

Nona Duffy

In far off Judea
  In Bethlehem town,
The little Christ Jesus
  From Heaven came down!
He came to a manger
  That first Christmas Day,
And slept on a blanket
  Spread out on the hay!

The shepherds looked on
  Or bent to adore Him;
And Wise-men came
  And knelt down before Him!
Bright angels announced
  The news of His birth,
And sang a loud anthem
  Of peace on the earth!

A star shone down softly
  Just over His head,
And Mary, His mother,
  Leaned over His bed!
The portals of Heaven
  Were open and bright,
While angels of glory
  Presided that night!

12

THE NATIVITY

Nona Duffy

It was nearly two thousand years ago
  The night of our Savior's birth,
That a bright star shone with a dazzling light
  And the angels sang on earth!
It was in a manger, rude and bare,
  That Jesus laid His head,
And with His mother, used the hay
  For pillow and for bed!

In Bethlehem, the babe was born,
  And a star showed where He lay;
The angels sang and shepherds came
  That first, glad Christmas Day!
And Wise-men in a caravan
  Saw the radiant star;
They packed some gifts in camel bags
  And followed from afar!

They found the holy family
  For they were Heaven sent;
They worshiped Him, then they returned
  To the distant Orient!
They told the news along the route
  And people spread the story
That the Messiah had been born
  To radiate God's glory!

THE DATE

Eldreth Russell

We sing of Jesus' birthday upon a
  silent night;
We read of that special village once
  filled with holy light;
Of narrow streets and busy, it's Bethlehem, they say,
So ancient, yet so modern, much like
  it is today.

The date is not important unless we
  worship too;
For Jesus came as God to man with
  love for me and you.
We must be born again, He said this
  long ago.
So if we trust, obey our Lord, eternal
  life we'll know.

THE WHOLE YEAR THROUGH

Phyllis Michael

The bells ring out on Christmas morn
"Christ is born! Christ is born!"
But tell me new, is this not true
The whole year through?

Then as we smile and gladly greet
Each friend and neighbor that we
  meet,
Let's all remember what we say
On Christmas Day.

"Glory to God in the highest and
  peace
To all and goodwill that shall never
  cease!"
Let's say it and say it and say it
  again,
"Peace to all men!"

CHRISTMAS LIVES

Helen Evans

Has Christmas lost all its meaning
  In the hurried times we share?
Has Christmas lost all its meaning
  With hatred seen everywhere?

Some would say it's all hoopla,
  That glittering lights hide the star,
But the calm of that first Christmas
  morning
  Can stay with us wherever we are.

Within the heart of each of us
  There's a special place for love;
A place to celebrate the joy
  Sent to us from Heaven above.

No, Christmas has not lost its
  meaning,
  We still sing the carols of old;
We still see the star through the
  glitter
  As we watch that story unfold.

No frantic pace will destroy it,
  For our Savior calms all our fears;
We'll always remember the Christ
  child,
  Christmas will live for all years.

A SAVIOR IS BORN

Phyllis Michael

Just why are folks singing?
And why are bells ringing?
  Just why is there love and good
    cheer?
The child in the manger,
The one some called stranger
  Is Jesus, our Savior so dear.

Above all the trappings
And bright-colored wrappings
  Of tissue and tinsel and bows,
There's one special greeting
That with each repeating
  The dearer and sweeter it grows.

A Savior is born,
Yes, our Savior is born!
  Christ Jesus, our Savior is born!
And that is the reason
For joy at this season,
  Christ Jesus, our Savior is born!

14

A SPECIAL NIGHT

Helen Evans

Christmas Eve is a special time
  A source of wonder fills the air;
Extra joy and gladness
  Surrounds us everywhere.

It's a time of preparation
  Of the gifts we are to give;
It's a time to recall the past
  Where the memories still live.

It's a time for family gatherings,
  To give thanks for all the mothers,
The fathers, uncles, aunts, and
    cousins,
  For the sisters and the brothers.

It's a time of overflowing
  With the love we radiate
When we remember the lowly
    manger
  What a magnificent holy date.

Christmas Eve is a special time,
  The night God gave us salvation;
May the message of this holy night
  Reach out and touch the nation.

I LOVE THE STORY

Nona Duffy

I love to hear the story
  Of that first Christmas night,
When shepherds watching grazing
    sheep
  Beheld a glorious light;
Of angels who announced the news,
  Of baby Jesus' birth;
Who told of one in swaddling
    clothes,
  To bring us peace on earth!

I love to hear about the star
  That led to where He lay,
And hovered over Bethlehem
  Upon that noted day!
I love to hear how shepherds came
  To see the infant child;
How loyal Joseph tended Him,
  And Mary, sweet and mild!

Of Wise-men who came riding in
  On camels from afar,
Across the desert, calm and still,
  And on bright gleaming star!
Let's sing of Mary and her Son,
  So innocent and small;
Who came to teach of love and
    peace,
  And to bring goodwill to all!

GLORY TO GOD

Phyllis Michael

I wish that I could have been there,
    too,
  The night the angels sang;
I wish that I could have heard their
    song,
  I'm sure the heavens rang.

I wish that I could have seen that
    star
  That shone so clear and bright;
I wish that I could have followed it
  And found the Christ that night.

But I can make Heaven ring tonight
  If I just do my part;
"Glory to God!" I'll shout and sing,
  "Christ is born within my heart."

CLOSER EACH CHRISTMAS

Helen Evans

I'm always thrilled at Christmas
  By the music and sounds I hear;
The beautiful music of Christmas
  Repeated year after year.

The children's angelic faces
  As they sing so heavenly;
Faces that I know tomorrow
  Will still mischievous be.

The story that heralds the coming
  Of Jesus, our Savior and friend;
The magnificent Bible story
  Showing love without an end.

Never, no never, will Christmas
  Grow old upon this earth,
For each year I'm drawn closer and
    closer
  As I celebrate His birth.

WAITING

Helen Evans

Christmas is a time of joyful waiting
  Expectation is everywhere,
Though hundreds of years have
    passed by
  The empty manger is there.

The soft hay still is near the cattle
  That will cradle and receive
The holy babe of Bethlehem,
  Salvation for all who believe.

In hope and trust we all await
  The coming of Christ's glory,
As once again we rejoice
  In the wondrous Christmas story.

NO TASK TOO LOWLY

Phyllis Michael

Oh, that I could have been that man
  Who brought the clean sweet hay
And placed it in the manger-bed
  Where Jesus was to lay.

I often wonder if he knew
  While working in the field,
Out there beneath the sun's warm
    rays
  Things God alone revealed.

I often wonder what he thought
  While placing hay just so
Upon that hard, cold stable floor;
  I wonder did he know

A precious little babe would be
  Without a soft, warm bed?
The King of all the world would need
  A place to lay His head.

I like to think he piled it high
  And smoothed it with his hand,
Perhaps not knowing why just then
  Except it was God's command.

Lest God choose me for some such
    task
  Somewhere along life's way,
May I do well the simple things
  That are my lot each day.

HEAVEN TOUCHED EARTH

Helen Evans

The night wind sifted through the
  cracks
  Of the stable on that night;
The air was crisp, the sky was clear
  That one star spread out a brilliant
  light.

On the hillside shepherds huddled
  close
  Keeping warm among the sheep,
When suddenly an angel came
  And aroused them from their sleep.

"I bring you tidings of great joy,
  Your Savior has been born!"
The shepherds went to Bethlehem
  That glorious Christmas morn.

The angel's promise had been kept
  For they saw dear Jesus' face;
God's only Son in swaddling clothes
  In this humble place.

Upon this Christmas long ago
  Heaven reached down from above
And gave to all the precious gift
  Of salvation through God's love.

CELEBRATION

Nona Duffy

In ten million homes this evening
  Christmas candles flame and flare!
But the crib that cradled Jesus
  Was a manger, crude and bare!
In cathedrals and in churches
  Choirs will carol for our King!
But the shepherds came at midnight
  And they heard the angels sing!

In ten million lighted cities
  Men will celebrate His birth;
Very few were there to greet Him
  When He came onto this earth.
Let's join the happy voices
  Let's clasp the outstretched hands,
Let's sing of peace and freedom
  With the folk of many lands!

THE CHRISTMAS STORY

Nona Duffy

One evening, over Bethlehem
  One certain star grew bright;
It led the Wise-men from afar
  That lovely Christmas night!
A Heavenly host of angels sang,
  And shepherds knelt in awe
To marvel at the wondrous song,
  And at the sight they saw!

The shepherds left and went in haste
  To find the little child
Within the stable at the inn
  With Mary, calm and mild.
The Wise-men came, led by the star,
  One night, in Bethlehem!
They knelt in worship at His feet,
  And brought their gifts to Him.

The sky was lit by radiance
  That made it bright as day,
And shone around the Christ child's
  head
  Asleep upon the hay.
And now again it's time to sing
  "Goodwill and peace on earth,"
And tell the story that we love
  Of Jesus and His birth!

CHRISTMAS STAR

Phyllis Michael

There are many Christmas lights to
see
But the ones I like best are the ones
on the tree.
I especially like the one at the top.
Oh, beautiful star, I can't help but
stop
Each time I pass, I just stand and
stare,
You look so very fine up there.

You're so much brighter and you're
up so high
At the very tip right next to the sky.
I know that's where Jesus, our
Savior, lives
I wonder, are you brighter because
He gives
His light to you? Shine on then, O
star,
Say, "Jesus sends His love to us
from afar."

HAPPY NEW YEAR

Nona Duffy

Belfry bells are loudly swinging
Old and young have joined in singing,
"Happy New Year! Happy New Year!
Happy New Year, everyone!"

It is now the midnight hour,
And from hall to belfry tower
Sounds the greeting, "Happy New
Year!
For the old year now is done!"

Happy hearts are gladly beating,
They extend a hearty greeting,
"Happy New Year! Happy New Year!
Happy New Year has begun!"

Horns are blowing, bells are pealing,
In our churches folks are kneeling,
Full of love and reverent feeling;
"Happy New Year, everyone!"

JUST ONE LITTLE BABY

Phyllis Michael

No palace to welcome the King of all kings,
No crown and no scepter of gold;
No bright royal robes for our Savior, no rings,
No feast in His honor I'm told.

No crowd to receive Him, no throng to adore,
No pillow to cradle His head;
No clothes but the cloths of some others He wore,
No cover to put on His bed.

Just one little baby, a manger of hay,
An inn and a star that shone bright,
Just one little baby, a mother and child,
But O, what the world gained that night!

READY FOR CHRISTMAS?

Kay Hoffman

"Are you ready for Christmas?"
 How lightly we ask
Amid the hustle and bustle
 Of holiday task.

But are we ready for Christmas?
 Truly ready for Him
Who came to the earth
 As the Savior of men?

Have we kept our hearts free
 Of the clutter of things
That hide the true meaning
 This blessed time brings?

Have we taken the time
 To meditate and pray,
Reflecting the wonder
 Of that first Christmas Day?

Oh, our homes may be ready
 With gifts to impart,
But are we ready for Christmas
 Deep down in our hearts?

CHRISTMAS SPIRIT

Kay Hoffman

If we could keep the spirit
 Of Christmas we hold dear,
We'd be a little kinder
 Each day throughout the year.

We'd find the time to pause
 Along our busy day
To lend a hand to someone
 Struggling on life's way.

If we could keep the spirit
 That prompts our Christmas living,
We'd be tolerant with others
 And a little more forgiving.

Fewer hearts would need be broken,
 More folks would wear a smile,
Not just because it's Christmas—
 But each day would be worthwhile.

If we could keep the spirit
 Of Christmas through the year,
We truly then would honor
 The Savior we hold dear.

THE FIRST CHRISTMAS

Nona Duffy

Jesus Christ, our Lord, was born
 In Bethlehem one day;
Some Wise-men brought rich gifts
    for Him,
 And shepherds came to pray!

If I had been a shepherd boy
 And lived near Bethlehem
I would have gone that Christmas
    Day
 And visited with Him!

I would have brought a lamb for
    Him,
 A warm and cuddly thing;
I would have tiptoed softly in
 And heard the angels sing!

EXERCISES

CHRISTMAS ECHOES

Helen Evans

Solo 1: I love Jesus, yes I do.
Solo 2: Me, too.
Solo 3: Me, too.
Solo 4: Me, too.
Solo 1: I like to sing for Jesus.
Solo 2: Me, too.
Solo 3: Me, too.
Solo 4: Me, too.
Solo 1: I like to go to Sunday school.
Solo 2: Me, too.
Solo 3: Me, too.
Solo 4: Me, too.
Solo 1: I like our Bible verses.
Solo 2: Me, too.
Solo 3: Me, too.
Solo 4: Me, too.
Solo 1: I think I hear an echo
Of everything I say;
I wish each one of you
A happy Christmas Day.
Solo 2: Me, too.
Solo 3: Me, too.
Solo 4: Me, too.

(Solo 1 grabs the three little ones and hurries off with them. They go off laughing because they have been three little pests. This selection would be a good one for an older child with three smaller sisters or brothers.)

20

WE'RE GLAD

Eldreth Russell

(For four children. Each holds a Bible.)

Child 1

I'm glad this Bible tells of love;
The love that Jesus came to share;
For He was born in Bethlehem
To save men everywhere.

Child 2

I'm glad this Bible tells of grace,
Like rain, His favors fall;
The manger held this Babe of grace
To try to save us all.

Child 3

I'm glad this Bible tells of one
The Wise-men said was king;
They gave their gifts to honor Him;
We give Him everything.

Child 4

I'm glad this Bible tells of one
The shepherds came to see;
For as a lamb He gave himself
To offer life to me.

All

We're glad the Bible came from God
And tells of Christmas Day;
This babe became the Son of Man,
The life, the truth, the way.

CHRISTMAS TODAY

Helen Evans

Solo 1: Tinsel and lights,
Solo 2: Carols and bells,
Solo 3: The story of Jesus
Solo 4: Our Bible tells.
Chorus: What does Christmas mean today?
Solo 5: Sleigh bells and snow,
Solo 6: Days of joy long ago,
Solo 7: Childhood's thrills,
Solo 8: Coasting down hills,
Chorus: What does Christmas mean today?
Solo 9: Moments of chatter,
Solo 10: No worries that matter,
Solo 11: Days filled with fun
Solo 12: For everyone.
Chorus: What does Christmas mean today?
Solo 13: Hustling and bustling
Solo 14: Through a jostling crowd,
Solo 15: Music blaring
Solo 16: So very loud!
Chorus: What does Christmas mean today? ·
Solo 17: Have we forgotten
Solo 18: Why we celebrate?
Solo 19: Is Jesus lost
Solo 20: On this special date?
Chorus: What does Christmas mean today?
Choir 1: Let's dedicate our lives anew,
Choir 2: With Jesus the center of all we do;
Chorus: Let's worship our God and often pray
Then we'll know the meaning of Christmas today.

IT'S CHRISTMAS

Helen Evans

Chorus: But the angel said to them,
Solo: Do not be afraid. I bring you good news of great joy that will be for all the people. Today in the town of David a Savior has been born to you; he is Christ the Lord.
Choir 1: The long-awaited day is here!
Chorus: It's Christmas!
Choir 2: The birth of Christ brings us cheer.
Chorus: It's Christmas!
Choir 1: The star of faith shines in the night.
Chorus: It's Christmas!
Choir 2: The star that gives a holy light.
Chorus: It's Christmas!
Choir 1: Again I hear the angels sing.
Chorus: It's Christmas!
Choir 2: The carols have a peaceful ring.
Chorus: It's Christmas!
Choir 1: Joy seems to beam from every face.
Chorus: It's Christmas!
Choir 2: Sending out God's love and grace.
Chorus: It's Christmas!
Solo: All glory to our Heavenly King!
Chorus: It's Christmas!

DON'T PACK JESUS AWAY

Helen Evans

Child 1
When Christmastime is over
And we've had a happy day;

Child 2
When we're packing decorations,
Let's not put Jesus away.

Child 3
Let's keep Jesus present always,

Child 4
Let's keep that same joy and cheer;
All
Then we'll have Christmas in our hearts
Each day of the grand new year!

WHEN IT'S CHRISTMAS

Helen Evans

Choir 1: Lovely greetings from everywhere,
Choir 2: A song of gladness fills the air,
Chorus: When it's Christmas.

Choir 1: Inspiration and faith we see,
Choir 2: Showing true love for humanity,
Chorus: When it's Christmas.

Choir 1: The church becomes the stable of love,
Choir 2: It seems that Christ comes down from above,
Chorus: When it's Christmas.

Choir 1: May love be with us again and again,
Choir 2: All through the year, not only—
Chorus: When it's Christmas.

WONDERFUL TIME

Helen Evans

Choir 1: Christmas is such a wonderful time
Choir 2: Filled with love for family;
Solo 1: A time for praise,
Solo 2: A time for love,
Solo 3: For everyone,
Solo 4: For me.

Choir 1: Christmas is such a wonderful time
Choir 2: Filled with love for others;
Solo 5: A time of joy,
Solo 6: A time of fun,
Solo 7: For me,
Solo 8: For sisters and brothers.

Choir 1: Christmas is such a wonderful time
Choir 2: Filled with love for friends;
Solo 9: A time to laugh,
Solo 10: A time to sing,
Solo 11: A time to worship our Heavenly king.

Choir 1: Christmas is such a wonderful time
Choir 2: The birth of a baby so dear;
Solo 12: Our Jesus,
Solo 13: Our Savior,
Solo 14: Our Lord!
Chorus: We're so happy when Christmas is here.

THANK YOU, GOD, FOR CHRISTMAS

Helen Evans

Solo 1: The star like a mirror
Shone on the hillside
Where frightened shep-
herds
Tried to run and hide.
Solo 2: "Fear not,"
Chorus: the angel said.
Solo 3: What could be stranger?
Solo 4: This child, the Christ, born
in a manger?
Solo 5: Could this be true?
Chorus: What a wondrous story!
Solo 6: Our Savior wrapped in
swaddling clothes?
Chorus: This holy one of glory?
Solo 7: Wise-men are traveling with
their earthly treasures?
Chorus: They go to seek the king?
Solo 8: Is this our holy Savior?
Chorus: Thank You, God, for that
Christmas night
When Your Son came to
earth;
For all the many blessings
given to all
By His humble birth.

A BABY IN A MANGER

C.R. Scheidies

Child 1
(Holds picture of manger scene.)
In His loving kindness
Jesus came to earth,
A baby in a manger,
A special virgin birth.

Child 2
(Holds picture of Jesus on the cross.)
He left His Heavenly throne,
To save us from loss,
As a baby in a manger,
As a Savior on a cross.

Child 3
(Holds picture of the risen Christ.)
So let us worship Him
Who came to bring release,
As a baby in a manger,
As Lord who gives us peace.

RING THE BELLS

C.R. Scheidies

Group One
Ring the bells of the steeple,
Ring them loud and clear.
Go tell the world our Lord arose!
Let's ring the bells this Easter.

Group Two
Ring out the news that Jesus lives
Today as long ago,
And though He died upon the cross,
He lives forevermore.

Group Three
He lives within my heart, 'tis true,
But He's as real as real can be;
The tomb just couldn't hold Him,
He arose to set us free.

Group Four
So let the bells ring out,
And tell the world Christ lives;
So everyone may come to Him
To receive the peace He gives.

23

DRAMA

GLORY TO GOD

A Christmas Program

Eldreth Russell

Characters:

Reader
Poet
Four shepherds
Three Wise-men
Joseph
Mary

Materials needed: Two silhouettes will be formed behind a sheet. You can use either a cardboard cutout or real people.

The organist should play Christmas carols or appropriate music during the whole program.

READER: The prophetic vision fell upon all willing men in ages past. Many were unwilling to listen, but God, with divine patience, kept on revealing until people listened and He was able to make known the fullness of His love and truth.

POET:

So close to God lived saints of old
  That in their hearts were formed a dream.
To them the Heavenly message told
  Of a coming one, the man supreme.
He'd live and love and light the light
  To brighten life with truth and right.

They told that Savior God would send
  To give to men a guiding hand,
When sin and war would finally end
  With love the fashion through the land.
The Holy Spirit from God's throne
  Made all this future vision known.

24

The prophets, sages, told of One
  Whose coming would assure the right,
In whom God's will would then be done,
  The Father's Son and His delight.
The Heavenly kingdom then would grow;
  This coming king would make it so.

Silhouette One: Wise-men

READER: Not only was the message of hope delivered by prophets but in this time of great expectation, God spoke through the heavens which again were declaring the glory of God.

POET:

While evil brought so many down
  With darkness leading men astray,
The Father charted a course of love
  To bring them to the lighted way.

A moving star placed in the sky
  Announced to man when Jesus came;
Star of the East, so bright and fair,
  The herald of His holy name.

The child divine of noble birth
  God's mission came to fill;
The Father gave His only Son
  To bring His truth and do His will.

READER: The star revealed to the Wise-men the birth of their king.

POET:

The Wise-men on their camels sat,
  Scanning far off western sky,
Where shone a bright and glistening star
  Inviting from its place on high.
Its rays were pointing down below
To Judea where now they'd go.

(Silhouette disappears as light is removed from the scene. The shepherds now walk to the middle of the scene, form a semicircle, and huddle together as if speaking to one another once in a while. No sound is made.)

READER: The heavens again declare the glory of God for an angel appears to these simple shepherds to tell them of the birth of the Savior.

(The light is now pointed upward toward the ceiling above the shepherds so they will look up. During this time, the angels appear behind the sheet so when the light is beamed at the sheet again, the angels appear.)

READER: The glory of the Lord appears to the shepherds, first with only one angel and then with a host of them. Their message was, "Do not be afraid. We bring you good news of great joy that will be for all the people. Today ... a Savior has been born to you." So the message of the coming Good Shepherd was made known to shepherds in the field. The host of angels then said, "Glory to God in the highest and peace on earth to men of good will."

POET:

Good news we bring
  To men of the earth;
Good news of joy
  In the Savior's birth.

In swaddling clothes
  In a manger will lay;
It is God in the flesh,
  Men will worship today.

(The light disappears. The silhouette is removed. Mary and Joseph form a new silhouette. Remember that the Wise-men came to a house, not the manger scene. The Reader can be reading during this change.)

READER: The Wise-men had been seeking the one who was born a king. Having lost the star, they came to Jerusalem and asked Herod about the birth of a child. The scribes told Herod that Bethlehem was the place where the Messiah would be born. As the Wise-men were sent on their way, they again saw the star and it led them to the house where Joseph and Mary were now staying.

(The Wise-men go before Joseph and Mary, and lay down their gifts as the poet speaks of each one.)

POET:

Before me is the one foretold;
As I would not from Him withhold,
I give to Him my gift of gold.

READER: There was no more costly gift to be given. How fitting that from this humble beginning, there would emerge the descendant of David who would sit on the throne and have an everlasting kingdom. It was gold for the king.

POET:

This gift of frankincense I share;
When burned will beautify the air
And blessed will be men everywhere.

READER: How fitting that this gift reminds us of priests who minister before the Lord and give their sacrifices to glorify Him. How reasonable to know that Jesus will be a priest forever, ever living to make intercession and to bless God's people.

POET:

The gift of myrrh can purify;
Prophetic, too, that He will die,
Yet through it all will glorify.

READER: Yes, indeed. His death will glorify God by revealing the love that was willing to give the very best gift possible. To think that God's love was that great and Jesus loved us so much He was willing to die for us.

(All the people gather around Mary, Jesus, and Joseph as the last reading is given. All join in singing "To God Be the Glory.")

READER: From this wonderful story has come the message of mercy to invite all men to become children of God. This is more than history. This is love come to life. Jesus was born among men, lived perfectly, suffered vicariously, died willingly, and arose victoriously. This offers salvation universally. We, too, must worship the Son and give our best to Him. First, we give ourselves and then what we have to honor Him. By faith, we follow Him and serve Him. Because we are justified by faith, we have peace with God through our Lord Jesus Christ: We also have access into His grace and rejoice in hope of the glory of God.

CLOSING: "O Come All Ye Faithful" (verse two)

THE GIFT OF THE BEASTS

Katherine Peavy

A Christmas playlet adapted
from a twelfth-century carol

Reader:

It's Christmas Eve in Bethlehem town
And all the stars in the sky shine down.

The baby Jesus lies asleep
Among the cattle and the sheep.

The Wise-men their gifts have given
And the angels have sung their carols from Heaven.

Now the beasts in the stable, by some good spell
Will tell of their gifts to Emmanuel.

Donkey:

I am the donkey, shaggy and brown
I carried His mother up hill and down;
I carried her safely to Bethlehem town,
I am the donkey, shaggy and brown.

Cow:

I am the cow all white and red,
I gave Him my manger for His bed;
I gave Him my hay to pillow His head,
I am the cow all white and red.

Sheep:

I am the sheep with the curly horn,
I gave Him my wool for His blanket warm,
To cover Him on Christmas morn;
I am the sheep with the curly horn.

Dove:

I am the dove in the rafters high
I cooed Him to sleep, my mate and I;
We cooed Him to sleep, we did not fly,
I am the dove in the rafters high.

Reader:

These gifts to Jesus, so strong and good,
Who was humbly born in a stable crude;
The friendly beasts have 'round Him stood,
'Round the blessed Jesus, so strong and good.

GOD'S CHRISTMAS GIFT

Eldreth Russell

(For eight children. Each carries one letter of the alphabet to spell "God's gift.")

G God is the Father who sent His Son
As a Christmas gift for everyone.

O Others should share this wonderful word
Like shepherds who told what they saw and heard.

D Dreams are for warnings to keep wise men free;
And Joseph and Mary were warned to flee.

S Shepherds saw angels that glorious night,
Bathed in the glory of Heavenly light.

G Gifts of great value we seldom see
Yet Jesus is priceless and He is free.

I Immanuel means God is walking with man;
In Bethlehem's story, new life began.

F "Fear not! Good tidings!" the angel said.
The coming of Jesus brings faith instead.

T Thanksgiving at Christmas? Yes, it is true;
We're thankful His gift is for me and you.

READING FOR CHRISTMAS

Helen Evans

Leader: The people walking in darkness have seen a great light.

Congregation: Jesus is the great light of our lives.

Leader: The angel said to them, "Do not be afraid. I bring you good news of great joy that will be for all the people.

Congregation: Jesus is the good news for all people everywhere.

Leader: Suddenly a great company of the heavenly host appeared with angel, praising God.

Congregation: Glory to God in the highest, and on earth, peace to men on whom his favor rests.

Leader: Jesus grew in wisdom and stature.

  Congregation: People who follow Jesus increase in knowledge and love of fellowman.

Leader: Be merciful, just as your Father is merciful.

Congregation: On this Christmas Day let us follow this Savior of the world and be merciful.

Leader: Let us light our candles and celebrate with joy the birth of Jesus, our Savior.

(The leader lights his candle. Then the leader lights the candle of the person on each side of the aisle. The flame is passed down the pew. When all candles are lighted, the congregation sings a carol as the choir moves slowly down the aisle. The congregation follows quietly, either with lighted or extinguished candles.)

COME TO JESUS

Ingrid Shelton

Characters:
  Mary
  Joseph
  Shepherds
  Wise-men
  Children

Setting: Mary and Joseph sit around manger with shepherds. Wise-men are standing behind them. Children stand to the side of manger.

FIRST CHILD:

> The shepherds came to Jesus when
> They heard the angel's word;
> They hastened to the manger
> And knelt before their Lord.
> *(Child kneels before manger.)*

SONG: Children, shepherds, and Wise-men sing "Away in a Manger."

SECOND CHILD:

> The Wise-men came to Jesus
> They came rich gifts to bring;
> They found the world's Messiah,
> And worshiped Christ the King.
> *(Child kneels before manger.)*

SONG: Same group sings "We Three Kings."

THIRD CHILD:

> I have come to Jesus,
> He's washed my sins away;
> And now I am so happy,
> I love Him more each day.
> *(Child kneels before manger.)*

SONG: Same group sings "O Come All Ye Faithful."

FOURTH CHILD:

> Will you come to Jesus?
> Give Him your life today?
> Accept Him as your Savior
> This Christmas, will you pray?
> *(Child kneels before manger.)*

SONG: All sing "Into My Heart."

A CHRISTMAS HEART

Cynthia Wilmoth

A Modern-day Play

Characters:

Nancy Allen —young Christian mother
Tina Allen —12-13 years old
Paula Evans —wealthy, slightly snobbish
Tommy Evans —12-13 years old
Mrs. Williams —young Christian mother
Sandy Smith —social worker
Helen Owens —non-Christian mother
Stacy Owens —12 years old
Karla Owens —9 years old
Jimmy Owens —7 years old
Lisa Owens —baby

Setting: It's Christmas Eve. A social worker is trying to find a family to take in another family whose house has burned down.

SCENE 1

(Interior of the Evans home. Paula Evans is busy in the living room. There is a knock at the door.)

PAULA EVANS *(answering the door)*: Why, Sandy, what a surprise to see you. Please come in.

SANDY SMITH: I'm sorry to bother you at this hour, Mrs. Evans, but I'm looking for someone to keep the Owens family this evening.

PAULA: Owens family ... isn't that the couple with all those children?

SANDY: They have four. A boy and three girls.

PAULA: Why are you looking for them somewhere to stay?

SANDY: Their house burned down this evening. I'm afraid they lost everything.

PAULA *(dryly)*: That's most unfortunate.

SANDY: Could you possibly let them spend the night with you? I know you have extra room.

PAULA *(gasping)*: Do you realize it's Christmas Eve? Why, I couldn't possibly take them this evening. I have a hundred things to do and all the family is coming for dinner tomorrow. I'm afraid I just can't. You understand, don't you?

SANDY: It seems I'll just have to keep looking. Perhaps the Williams family can help.

PAULA: Splendid idea! I'm sure the Owenses would be better off there anyway. Merry Christmas, Sandy.

SANDY *(sadly)*: Merry Christmas indeed. Goodbye Paula. *(Sandy exits. Lights out.)*

(Set up the Williams home. Mrs. Williams is either busy in the living room or comes from offstage when doorknock sounds.)

MRS. WILLIAMS *(answering the door)*: Sandy, hello. Please come in.

SANDY: No, I can't stay to visit. I'm here to ask a favor.

MRS. WILLIAMS: What is it you need?

SANDY: You know the Owens family?

MRS. WILLIAMS: Of course.

SANDY: Well, their house burned down this evening. They need a place to stay.

MRS. WILLIAMS: How awful for them. Well, I'd love to help if I could, but I don't have any extra space for them all. I could take a couple of the children perhaps.

SANDY: I was trying to keep them together. It's Christmas Eve and a family should be together.

MRS. WILLIAMS: I simply couldn't take them all. I have my own family to think of. You understand, don't you?

SANDY: Of course. Well, I'd better be on my way. Thanks for your time.

MRS. WILLIAMS: Let me know if there is anything else I can do.

SANDY: All right. Goodbye. *(Sandy exits. Lights out.)*

(Set up the Allen home. Mrs. Allen is busy in the living room. Knock sounds at door.)

NANCY ALLEN *(answering the door)*: Sandy, what are you doing out on a night like this? Come in.

SANDY: Thanks, Nancy. *(They move onstage and sit down.)* I'm so sorry to bother you on Christmas Eve like this, but you're my last hope.

NANCY: Sounds serious. What's the problem?

SANDY: It is serious and I can't seem to find anyone willing to help. I know you don't really have the room, but I need a place for the Owens family to stay. Their house burned down this evening and they lost everything.

NANCY: Oh, no, how terrible! Of course they can stay here. We can find room for them all. You should have come here first, Sandy.

SANDY: I guess so. Paula has the most room but she wouldn't do it because of her big family dinner, and Mrs. Williams offered to take a couple of the children, but in light of things—it being Christmas and all—I thought they should be together.

NANCY: Of course, I agree. Where are they now?

SANDY: Waiting for me to pick them up. I know the extra work this will be for you, Nancy, and I apologize for causing you any trouble.

NANCY: Nonsense. I'm glad to help.

SANDY: I knew I could count on you. I'll go get them now. Thanks a lot. *(Sandy exits. Nancy turns to find Tina, her daughter, standing there.)*

NANCY: Did you hear what Sandy wanted?

TINA: Yes. How terrible to lose your home like that and especially on Christmas Eve.

NANCY: Those poor little children.

TINA: Mom, I think it's awful that Mrs. Evans wouldn't keep them. She has that huge house. What a snob! She thinks she's better than anyone.

NANCY: Now, Tina, we mustn't be too critical of Mrs. Evans. She always has that big family dinner on Christmas Day.

TINA: All the same, it seems nasty to turn a family out in the cold like that. She makes the innkeeper at Bethlehem look like Mr. Nice Guy.

NANCY: I think she has more compassion than you realize.

TINA: You're just too nice to criticize anyone, Mom. *(Pauses thoughtfully.)* You know, those kids aren't going to have any presents for Christmas. How about me wrapping my doll to give to little Karla.

NANCY: What a good idea. I've been trying to think of something to give them all. Maybe Stacy could have one of your dresses. You're about the same size. But something for Jimmy ... that's going to be difficult. Let's think about it while we get the cot set up in your room and get the extra beds ready. *(Both exit.)*

SCENE 2

(Sandy is bringing the Owens family to the house. The children are in pajamas and wrapped in blankets.)

NANCY *(answering the door):* Please, come in.

SANDY: Nancy, you remember Helen Owens, and this is Stacy, Karla, Jimmy, and Lisa.

HELEN OWENS: I'm sorry to be a burden to you and I can't thank you enough for taking us in.

NANCY: That's all right. I'm glad I can be of help.

JIMMY: Are we going to sleep in your barn?

HELEN *(rebuking):* Jimmy!

SANDY: That's okay, Helen. I'm afraid that's my fault. I was telling the children on the way over here about the night Jesus was born. Mary and Joseph couldn't find anywhere to stay and Jesus was born in a stable. I guess Jimmy thought he was going to end up in a stable, too!

NANCY: Absolutely not, Jimmy. You have a nice warm cot in the next room. Tina, why don't you show the children to their room. I'm sure you all must be tired. *(Tina and children exit.)*

HELEN: Yes, we all are. My husband will be coming over later.

SANDY: Well, I'll be on my way. I'll stop over tomorrow with some food and things.

NANCY: Okay, Sandy.

SANDY: Thanks again, Nancy. Goodnight everyone. *(Exits.)*

NANCY *(turning to Helen):* Here, let me show you where you can rest. *(Both exit.)*

SCENE 3

(Stacy, Karla, and Jimmy come onstage and go up to tree. Lights are dimmed or off except for tree lights.)

KARLA: It's so pretty!

JIMMY: Look at all the presents!

KARLA *(bending down and picking up package):* Look, Stacy! This has my name on it.

STACY: Karla, put that down! Come on now, you've seen the tree and we have to go back to bed.
(Tina enters.)

TINA: Did you all need something?

STACY *(hesitantly):* No, they're just so excited about Christmas and they wanted to see the tree. We're sorry.

TINA: Oh, don't be. That's okay. I love to look at the tree, too.

KARLA *(looking at nativity scene under tree):* Isn't this the baby Jesus that Mrs. Smith was telling us about tonight?

TINA: Yes.

JIMMY: Why do you have it under the tree?

TINA: That's to help us remember why we celebrate Christmas. The most important thing to remember is that God's gift to us was baby Jesus.

STACY: But if we're supposed to be celebrating Jesus' birthday, why do we get the presents?

TINA: Mostly because over the years people have forgotten what Christmas is really about. People think more about getting things than they do giving. But as we give gifts to one another, it should remind us of God's gift to us.

STACY: But why did He send His Son?

TINA: I guess an easy way to answer that would be what my Sunday school teacher taught me. "For God so loved the world that he gave his one and only Son, that whoever believes in him should not perish but have eternal life." He showed us His love by coming and dying for us.

KARLA: Does He love me, too?

TINA: Yes, Karla, He loves all of us.

NANCY *(entering):* Why are you children still up?

TINA: We were just talking.

NANCY: Well, I think it's way past bedtime.

(Children go offstage saying goodnight. Nancy hears a knock at the door. Upon opening the door, she sees Mrs. Evans and Tommy with several boxes and sacks.)

NANCY: Paula, what a surprise!

PAULA: May we come in, Nancy?

NANCY: Yes, please do.

PAULA: We're sorry to disturb you at this hour.

NANCY *(pointing to boxes):* What is all this?

TOMMY *(very excited):* It's food and presents for the Owens family. And Mrs. Williams sent some clothing, too.

NANCY: Well, I don't know what to say.

PAULA: I want to apologize, Nancy. I'm ashamed of myself. I didn't realize I was being so selfish until Tommy started talking about the children not having any presents and how bad it made him feel.

TOMMY: I brought a train and some cars to give to Jimmy. And there's candy for everyone.

PAULA: I called Sandy back to tell her that I'd changed my mind and would keep them, but she said they were already at your house. We'd like to help in some way too, so we brought these things over. Tomorrow I want you to bring the Owens family to my house for Christmas dinner.

NANCY: You don't have to do that.

PAULA: I insist that you *all* come. You *know* there will be enough food for everyone. Please, come.

NANCY *(hesitantly):* If you're sure, we'd be delighted.

PAULA: Good! We'll see everyone at noon.

TOMMY: And don't be late. I'm getting hungry just thinking about all the food.

PAULA: Let's go, Tommy. Merry Christmas, Nancy.

NANCY: Merry Christmas to you, Paula, and thanks so much.

(Paula and Tommy exit.)

TINA: I can't believe it Mom! Look at all this stuff, and tomorrow we're eating at the Evans' house.

NANCY: Maybe you were wrong about Mrs. Evans.

TINA *(slowly):* Well, maybe. It looks like the true spirit of Christmas has shone through. Let's hope she keeps it the whole year.

NANCY *(smiling):* Let's hope we all do, Tina. All of us need that spirit of love every day. Just think of the difference in our families, the church, and even the world if we all truly had a Christmas heart. Now, let's try and get some sleep. Tomorrow is a *big* day.

LET PRAISE RING OUT

Ada Tomlinson

Let praise ring out wherever you are,
  Wherever you go or stay,
As angels from the realms above,
  Even on a rainy day.

All creatures here below give
    praise—
  The mountains, trees, and sea—
The moon, the stars give praise to
    God,
  So why shouldn't you and me?

MAKE ME WORTHY

Helen Evans

I give myself to You, dear Lord,
  On this Thanksgiving Day.
I know that You are with me
  All along the way.

You know my every need, dear Lord;
  You send blessings from above.
I know that You are watching
  And guiding me with love.

I'll work for You, dear Lord,
  And this I truly pray;
Make me worthy of You
  On this Thanksgiving Day.

BE THANKFUL

Mary Jenkin

Let us all be thankful
  That in our land we're free
To go to church, to honor God,
  To serve Him happily!

Let us all be thankful
  That we can have a share
In telling others of our God
  Who loves folks everywhere.

NOW IS THE TIME

Neva Baker

Now is the time to be thankful;
  Now is the time to give praise;
Now is the time to help someone in
    need;
  Now—not "one of these days."

Now is the time to give someone a
    hand,
  Or kind words, or a quarter of pie.
If we wait 'til next year, they may not
    be here;
  Or—we might put it off 'til we die.

COUNT THE BLESSINGS

Dorothy Stroud

If we would count the blessings
  God gives to each of us,
There'd be no time for grumbling,
  Nor time to fret and fuss!

We'd be so busy thanking
  The Lord, the whole day through,
That happiness would bubble up
  And make our hearts all new!

PILGRIMS WERE THANKFUL

Dorothy Stroud

The Pilgrims were thankful
  For harvest of grain,
For food from the forest,
  For sunshine and rain.

If they could be thankful
  For their scanty store,
Then we should be thankful,
  For we have much more.

MAKE EVERY DAY A
THANKFUL DAY

Lillian Beck

Thanksgiving Day is filled
  With notes of joyous praise,
But in our busy lives
  We take the other days
And use them thoughtlessly
  As they pass one by one;
Sometimes we fail to speak
  Our thanks when day is done.
When we show gratitude
  In all we do and say,
Then every day will be
  A blest Thanksgiving Day.

PRAY WITH YOUR HEART

Pearl Turner

A little boy sat in his church one day.
He heard the music and wanted to
  pray.
But words wouldn't come, he just
  couldn't start,
So he used not his lips, but prayed
  with his heart.

Now if you are thankful for your
  mother's care,
For sunshine and flowers and all
  that is fair;
Yes, if you feel thankful on Thanksgiving Day,
Just lift up your heart and you'll
  learn how to pray.

MY CALENDAR

Margaretta Harmon

  (Carries a big calendar.)
God gives us so many days
  (Flips pages of calendar.)
To spend in lots of pleasant ways.
It isn't fair to use but one
  (Points to Thanksgiving.)
To thank Him for all He has done.

This year I know what I shall do,
  (Points to self.)
And I suggest you do it too;
  (Points to audience.)
Let's thank the Father every day
  (Flips the calendar.)
For blessings that He sends our way.

THE BEST SEASON

Samuel Cox

Leaves, all colored, start to fall.
Autumn is the best of all.
Soon she makes a lovely nest
For the winter's peaceful rest.

Such a pretty season too;
Lots and lots of things to do!
Dig potatoes, haul them in;
Put the apples in the bin!

Happy voices! Running feet,
Knowing where to go to eat!
It's no wonder Christians say,
"What a fine Thanksgiving Day!"

HELP ME TO REMEMBER

Verna Rose

I saw a little bird
  Way up in a tree;
And as I looked right up at him
  He looked down at me.

He looked so very happy,
  Then he began to sing;
He seemed to be so thankful
  For life and everything.

And then I said, "Dear Jesus,
  Just help me to be
As very, very thankful
  As that bird up in the tree.

"Help me to remember
  That I need never fear,
For You will always care for me,
  My Lord and Savior dear."

ALL SEASON'S GIFTS

Daisy Clay

For violets in the springtime,
  For roses all summer long,
For blue sky spattered with white
    clouds,
  For the birds with their beautiful
    song.
For the bright-colored leaves in the
    autumn,
  For red apples ripe on the tree,
For a snow-covered world in winter,
  Our thanks, dear Father, to Thee.

THANKSGIVING EVERY DAY

Margaretta Harmon

I think it's such a shame to wait
  For just one day a year
To bow my head above my plate
  And thankfulness make clear.

It seems to me that every day
  God wants my thanks expressed;
So every day, "Thank You," I'll say,
  Since daily I am blessed.

THE FARMERS' THANK-YOU

Mary Poole

Trees are decked in gold and red,
Bright blue skies are overhead.
Harvesting is now all done,
Well-earned rest of earth begun.
So we gladly gather here
To thank God for our fruitful year.

SO MUCH

Helen Evans

God has given us so much:
  The sun, the rain, the snow;
He has made the world we see,
  Its beauty we all know.

God only asks we follow Him;
  Our love now let us bring,
And give our hearts to Jesus,
  As little children sing.

THANKSGIVING HEARTS

Louise Novotny

Thanksgiving hearts are always filled
  With peace and hope and joy,
Bringing most delightful smiles
  To every girl and boy.

Thanksgiving hearts are always filled
  With abundant love,
Making this old earth quite like
  The lovely Heav'n above.

A FINE MOTHER

Helen Evans

I have the nicest mother,
  She lets me help her bake;
I make candy, pie, and cookies,
  And sometimes even cake.

I like to measure out the flour,
  I like to stir and stir;
My mother says I'm really good
  And so much help to her.

When Thanksgiving Day is near
  Our days are extra fine;
I hope you have fun at your house
  With a mother dear as mine.

BE THANKFUL

Mary Jenkin

Let us all be thankful
  That in our land we're free
To go to church, to honor God,
  To serve Him happily!

Let us all be thankful
  That we can have a share
In telling others of our God
  Who loves folk everywhere.

THANK THE LORD

Vida Nixon

Thank the Lord for safety,
Bringing Pilgrims o'er the sea,
And for making hearts so brave
As to baffle angry wave.
Thank Him for the faith of men
Strong enough for trusting, when
Tempest battled with the sail,
And their bark was light and frail.

Thank the Lord for motives pure
In those hearts that did endure
Hardships for their freedom's right
And looked not for burdens light.
Thank Him for foundation laid,
And for everything that made
Of the Puritan's estate
This, our country, great.

Thank the Lord for men of might
Who stood for their country's right.
Thank Him for the hand of love
That directed from above,
And, through all adversity,
Kept a nation glad and free.
For our church and state and store
Thank the Lord for evermore.

TRUE THANKFULNESS

Dorothy Stroud

True thankfulness just seems to be
As natural as day to me.
For there are, oh, so many things
That almost make my heart take
    wings!
I'm thankful, most of all, that we
Can gather here to worship Thee,
And thankful for our daily bread,
For by Your hand we're amply fed.
Dear Lord, on this Thanksgiving Day,
In humbleness and love we pray
That You will bless and keep us true
Another safe and glad year through!

THANKSGIVING BLESSING

Lois Sink

Cranberries, turkey, and pumpkin pie,
    Lots of good things to eat,
Spread out on the table in great
    array
    Make for a feast complete.

Let's pause for a moment and bow
    our heads
    While we thank our Father above
For giving us richly all things to
    enjoy—
    How great is His wonderful love!

THANKSGIVING TIME

Gano Karns

Thanksgiving is
A time of giving thanks to God,
Whose mighty hand prepared the
    sod
And sent the sunshine and the rain
That grows and ripens golden grain.

A time of praise to Him above
Who sends His blessings and His
    love,
That all His creatures here below
Might know the love He does bestow.

A time to count our blessings all,
Though they be great or only small.
To thank our Father for each one,
And most especially, for His Son.

THANKSGIVING

Gano Karns

Thanksgiving is a time of praise
    And thanks to God above
For all the good things He bestows
    And for His boundless love.

Thanksgiving is a time to share
    The bounties we receive
With those who are less fortunate
    And those who are in need.

Thanksgiving is a time of joy,
    A time to sing and pray;
It need not be just once a year,
    But each and every day.

I'M THANKFUL EVERY DAY

Lucile Sleigh

Thanksgiving comes but once a year;
Some folks are glad but once, I fear.
But Christians like we are, I say,
Should be thankful every day!

Suppose the Lord forgot us all,
Nor listened to us when we call,
Except on one day of the year,
How sad we'd feel, and full of fear!

So I've decided it is right
To give Him thanks both day and
     night
And every single time I pray,
As well as on Thanksgiving Day.

THANKSGIVING

Frank Sherman

For morning and the hopes of day,
For hours to work and hours to play,
For courage and contentment here,
For trust to strengthen, joy to cheer,
We praise You, Lord!

For evening and the duties done,
For every strife of conscience won,
For hours to dream and hours to rest,
For all Your love made manifest,
We bless You, Lord.

For home and those who love us
     there,
For friends and kindred everywhere,
For life that is and life to be,
Eternal fellowship with Thee
We thank You, Lord.

LOVE AND CARE

Elizabeth Haynes

We thank You for Your love and care,
And all blessings that You send.
But most of all we thank You
For our Savior, who is our friend.

DON'T YOU?

Elizabeth Haynes

Every grown-up person
   And all the children, too,
Thank the Lord for all He's done—
   I surely do, don't you?

All the precious children
   And all the grown-ups, too
Praise the Lord for loving us—
   I surely do, don't you?

MAKE MELODY

Ada Tomlinson

Make melody in your heart
   Three hundred sixty-five days each
     year.
Give God an offering of praise
   And He will draw very near.

Thank God at all times for His
   blessings,
   And sing when the day seems long.
Every gift from above is so precious,
   Especially the gift of song.

OUR DAY

Phyllis Michael

(Hands in attitude of prayer)
Today is OUR day, you know,
The one where we say and show
(Holds up card saying "Thank you, God.")
Thank You, dear God above
For all those folks we love.

THE TURKEY

Peggy Kinney

The turkey's in the oven,
  Stuffed and getting brown.
Grandmother and Grandfather
  Are driving out from town.
Seems everyone is coming!
  I hope that they can see
One drumstick on that turkey
  Is meant for little me!

GOD IS

Phyllis Michael

God is great,
  God is strong,
And He'll keep me
  From all wrong.

God is true,
  God is kind
And no better
  Friend you'll find.

FOR MANY THINGS

Helen Evans

We thank You, God, for many things,
  Things we so often forget;
The sunshine on the hillside,
  The grass from showers still wet.

For little puppies, kittens, ducks,
  For clouds that float along;
For birds that flutter in the trees
  And sing a cheerful song.

We thank You, God, for many things,
  For the joy You've given, too;
May we be thankful always
  And try to live like You.

FROM HEARTS SINCERE AND TRUE

Dorothy Stroud

We really don't deserve the things
  So wonderful and good
That God sends freely to us all;
  But don't you think we should
Give Him our words of grateful
  praise
  From hearts sincere and true?
I'm sure His blessings then will fall
  On everyone of you!

MY HEART SINGS OUT

Louise Novotny

My heart sings out in thanks
  For all that You have done;
For all the blessings I enjoy,
  For the gift of Your dear Son.

My heart sings out in peace
  That comes from God above,
That fills my soul with perfect rest,
  Peace—gift of God's great love.

My heart sings out in faith
  Unwavering and tried.
Faith that removes mountains high
  And in You does abide.

My heart sings out in love
  For what You are to me.
You are my life, my strength, my all—
  I give myself to Thee.

Sing on, O thankful heart,
  Cheer others on their way.
Do not wait to sing tomorrow
  Begin, my heart, today.

THANKSGIVING FOR THESE LIGHTS

Mary Whipple

For little bits of light that blink
  And wink about the sky,
For little bits of sparkly lights
  That are in my mother's eye,

For the round sun that turns and
    burns
  And fills the world with light,
For moon that outlines silvery,
  Lovely hills within the night,

For feathery bits of light when
  Snowflakes fly and skip and nod,
For all these things You've given us
  From high, I thank You, God.

THANKFUL FOR THE HARVEST

Neva Baker

When the Lord of the bountiful
    harvest
  Gives His gifts to the children of
    men,
It's the time to give thanks and be
    grateful—
  It's time of Thanksgiving again.

For the corn and the beans and
    potatoes,
  For the cabbage and pumpkin and
    beet,
For the squash and the turnip and
    carrot,
  For the oats and the barley and
    wheat.

For the apples and peaches and
    cherries,
  For the prune and the plum and the
    pear,
For the grapes and the melons and
    berries,
  For the honey and nuts we may
    share.

To the Lord of the bountiful harvest
  Go the thanks of the children of
    men,
That the pantry and cellar and store-
    house
  Are replenished with food once
    again.

LAND OF BOUNTEOUS GRACE

Nixon Waterman

O ripe, round year! Like a mellowed rhyme
  Told in the twilight's dew and dusk,
Rich with the scent of rose and thyme,
  Blended with the garden's mint and musk,
Is the harvest song when the tasks are done
  And the autumn fields of brown and gray
Are sombered signs of the riches won
  For the joy of glad Thanksgiving Day.

April, coy, with a dash of rain
  (Tears of joy from her sunny eyes,)
Hiding her face in a silver skein,
  And a rainbow gladding all the skies!
May, in her comely beauty blest,
  Putting the good, kind earth in tune.
Then field and forest richly dressed
  In the fairest, rarest robes of June.

Then comes July with her ardent rays,
  And over the earth a ripeness steals,
'Til, with her lingering langorous ways
  Comes August yellowing all the fields.
Then bright September reigns her while,
  'Til brown October holds her sway,
And then November, wreathed in smiles,
  Comes bringing the glad Thanksgiving Day.

Seed and soil and sun and shower,
  Each one adding his happy part,
Bringing the gifts of fruit and flower,
  But best of all is a thankful heart.
A thankful heart that is quick to trace
  The golden blessings along the way—
That leads through the land of bounteous grace
  To the joy of glad Thanksgiving Day.

I GIVE MY THANKS TO THEE

Mildred Phillips

There is a church in our town
  That is very dear to me,
For this place to worship, Lord,
  I give my thanks to Thee.

I have a Holy Bible;
  It means so much to me;
For this, Your Word of truth, Lord,
  I give my thanks to Thee.

I have a Lord and Savior,
  He took my sins from me;
For this, Your precious Son, Lord,
  I give my thanks to Thee.

I have the promise of Heaven
  If true to Him I'll be,
For this our hope of life, Lord,
  I give my thanks to Thee.

GOD ONLY ASKS OUR GRATITUDE

Mary Poole

How many things God makes to grow
From small brown bulbs and seeds
  we sow;
Red tulips, yellow daffodils,
Green blades of wheat on spring-
  warm hills.

How many notes God gives the birds
That thrill us more than songs with
  words;
How many clouds to scurry by,
How many stars to wink on high.

How many butterflies and bees,
How many green and swaying trees,
How many dawns with rose-gold
  light,
How many sunsets flaming bright.

We cannot list the things that be,
Our Father's gifts to you and me;
And for this countless multitude
God only asks our gratitude.

I THANK THEE

Maribelle Eucks

For eyes to see the morning sun,
For rest when all my tasks are done,
For feet to roam the woodland ways,
For peace to grace my earthly days,
I thank Thee.

For friends I know and love as one,
For goals well set and finally won,
For water where the moonlight plays,
For campfires and their magic blaze,
I thank Thee.

For strength to conquer tasks begun,
For health to swim and play and run,
For faith in prayer my heart to raise,
For voice to sing a grateful praise,
I thank Thee.

SETTING THE TABLE

Katherine Peavy

(A playlet for two children)

Thanksgiving Day again is here
One of the happiest days of the year.

It's such a joyous holiday
We'll help Mother instead of play.

We'll spread the cloth upon the table
As nice and neat as we are able.

We'll place the silver and glasses and then
We'll set the table up for ten.

There's our parents, our brother, and our sisters,
And Gramps and Gram and dear Aunt Esther.

There's you and me and Uncle Steven
And Cousin John—that makes a dozen!

We'll lay the napkins and pour the water,
Put on the rolls and then the butter.
Now that the table looks so neat
Thanksgiving dinner will be a treat.

I'm thankful for so many things
That Thanksgiving Day always brings.

I'm thankful for so much nice food,
And I'm thankful that it is so good.

And we should thank God the whole year through
For gifts of home and family, too!

RICHLY BLESSED

Helen Evans

Choir 1: We are richly blessed in so many ways;

Choir 2: We have talents and abilities for which we give God praise.

Choir 1: We are richly blessed with a home filled with love,

Choir 2: Where we worship together and receive blessings from above.

Choir 1: We are richly blessed! There is beauty on this earth;

Choir 2: The sunrise in the morning gives each day new birth.

Chorus: We are richly blessed!
Solo 1: We have eyes to see and ears to hear.

Chorus: So on this Thanksgiving Day we thank God who is ever near.

GOD'S GIFTS

Helen Evans

Child 1

God has given us beautiful skies
And eyes that we may see;
He has given us voices that sing
And ears to hear the melody.

Child 2

God has given us lovely hands
That we may do useful things;
That we may play musical
instruments
And know the joy that brings.

Child 3

God has given us faces
That can smile the troubles away,
So let's be very thankful
And serve Him every day.

THANKSGIVING

Peggy Kinney

T is the **turkey,** a noble bird,
H is for **how** he gets done;
A is for **all** who'll be coming to eat,
N is for what's left—that's **none.**
K is for **kids** who'll have a good time,
S is for **songs** that we'll sing;
G is for **grace** said before we eat,
I is for **ice cream** and things.
V is for **victory** we have through our Lord,
I is the **indwelling**—the Holy Ghost;
N is for **newness** when we come to Him,
G is for **God,** we thank Him the most.